IF YOU LOVE VIDEO GAMES, YOU COULD BE...

By Thea Feldman
Illustrated by Natalie Kwee

Ready-to-Read

SIMON SPOTLIGHT

An imprint of Simon & Schuster Children's Publishing Division • 1230 Avenue of the Americas, New York, New York 10020
This Simon Spotlight edition May 2019 • Text copyright © 2019 by Simon & Schuster, Inc. • Illustrations copyright © 2019 by
Natalie Kwee • All rights reserved, including the right of reproduction in whole or in part in any form. SIMON SPOTLIGHT,
READY-TO-READ, and colophon are registered trademarks of Simon & Schuster, Inc. For information about special discounts
for bulk purchases, please contact Simon & Schuster Special Sales at 1-866-506-1949 or business@simonandschuster.com.
Manufactured in the United States of America 0122 LAK • 4 6 8 10 9 7 5 • Library of Congress Cataloging-in-
Publication Data • Names: Feldman, Thea, author. | Kwee, Natalie, illustrator. Title: If you love video games, you could be . . .
/ by Thea Feldman ; illustrated by Natalie Kwee. Description: Simon Spotlight edition. | New York, New York : Ready-to-Read,
Simon Spotlight, 2019. | Series: If you love... | Audience: Age 5-7. Identifiers: LCCN 2018043075 | ISBN 9781534443983 (pbk.) |
ISBN 9781534443990 (hardcover) | ISBN 9781534444003 (eBook) • Subjects: LCSH: Video games—Design—Vocational
guidance—Juvenile literature. | Video games industry—Vocational guidance—Juvenile literature. | Video games—Author-
ship—Vocational guidance—Juvenile literature. | Video games—Programming—Vocational guidance—Juvenile literature.
Classification: LCC GV1469.3 .F45 2019 | DDC 794.8—dc23 LC record available at https://lccn.loc.gov/2018043075

Glossary

Animation: a way of using technology to make images move and come to life on a screen

Code: a set of instructions written for computers to understand

Computer bug: an error that prevents a computer from working the way that it should

Dialogue: a conversation between two or more characters

Motion capture: technology that records a human's movements and changes them into computer-animated images

Role-playing game: a game where players pretend to be characters that go on different adventures

Storyboard: a group of panels with pictures and words that are organized to tell a story

Video game animator: an artist who uses technology to make images move on a screen

Video game designer: a person who comes up with the story, rules, and other ideas for a video game

Video game programmer: a person who writes computer code in order to make a game work

Video game writer: a person who writes the words that appear in a game, like dialogue and instructions

Note to readers: Some of these words may have more than one definition. The definitions above are how these words are used in this book.

CONTENTS

Introduction

Do you love playing video games?
If so, you know that anything
is possible when you're gaming.
You can solve puzzles,
fight monsters,
and even build imaginary worlds.

Did you know that some people get to work on video games every day? When you grow up, you could help make video games like they do!

Chapter 1:
Video Game Writer

Do you like video games
with great stories?
Then you might want to be
a video game writer!

Video game writers are in charge of the words that appear in a game. Before they start writing, though, sometimes they talk through what the story is about with the video game designers.

Writers are especially important
for role-playing games that have
many characters and adventures.
On these projects,
there may be more than one writer.

They may answer questions like "Who is the main character?" and "Where does the story take place?" They use their imaginations to come up with all those ideas.

Sometimes writers and designers
use a storyboard, which is
a set of pictures and words
arranged to tell a story.
This helps them plan
and organize their ideas.

When they are happy with the story, the writers create the dialogue (say: DYE-uh-log), or the words that the characters say.

They also write hints and
instructions that appear
in the game, like
"Press B to jump" and
"Run away from the dragon!"

If you want to be a video game writer, you can prepare by reading a lot of books and writing your own stories. What kind of stories would you like to tell?

Chapter 2:
Video Game Animator

Whoosh! Zoom! Zip!
One of the most exciting parts of
a video game is its action.

A video game animator uses special computer programs to bring the game to life.

An animator pays attention
to details. For example,
when a character talks, the animator
makes sure that the lips move to
match what they are saying.

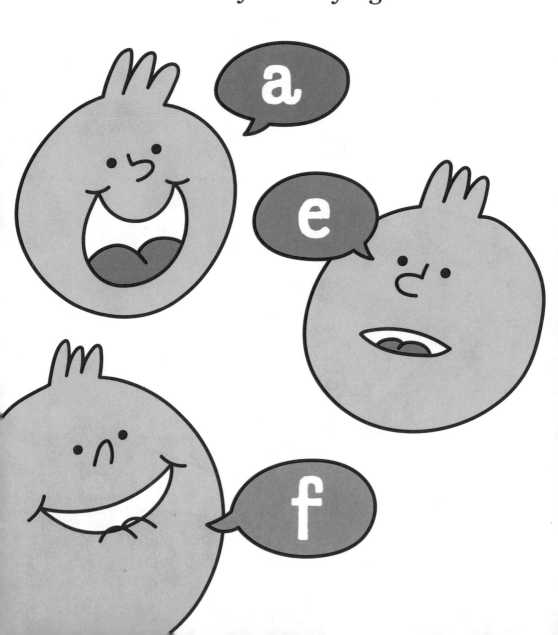

Animators also figure out
how long the actions should last.
If it only takes two seconds to talk,
the character's mouth should not
move for six seconds!

The animator also uses a lot of math. When they first create a character on a computer, they build it out of many small shapes.

They decide on the number of shapes to use and how to arrange them. A single arm can be made out of hundreds of shapes!

Some animators work with motion capture, where a person wears a special suit. Then they move around while a computer records each movement. The animator uses those videos as a guide to make their characters move like real people.

Characters are not the only things
that animators bring to life.
They work on anything that moves,
like shooting stars or zooming cars.

If you want to be a video game
animator, you can start by drawing
things that move.
Look closely at a flying bird.
How do its wings move?
Keep your eyes open,
and you can become an expert
on movement!

Chapter 3:
Video Game Programmer

How does all the creative work of writers and animators become a game you can actually play? Video game programmers make that happen!

Video game programmers are sometimes called developers. They make everything in the game work the way that it should.

They do that by writing code, which is a set of instructions that tells computers what to do. It is written in special languages made just for computers.

Each and every video game, whether played on a laptop or in an arcade, needs code to work properly.

Imagine a game where you need to dodge bananas in order to stay alive. The programmer writes code that says,
"If the character touches a banana, decrease its health by one heart."

Then if you touch a banana, the game follows the instructions and takes one heart away. In this way a programmer tells the game *exactly* what to do!

Programmers spend a lot of time fixing computer bugs, or errors, that prevent the game from working. It takes a lot of patience to write code!

If you want to be a video game programmer, there are many books, websites, and even video games about coding.
It is never too early to start learning. Give it a try!

How would you like to write the story, animate the characters, or develop the code for the next popular video game?

Many different people work together to create a game. They all have one thing in common, though. They love gaming, just like you!

Video game writer, animator, and programmer are just a few of the cool careers for people who want to make video games. Turn the page to discover even more jobs!

More Video Game Jobs

A **video game producer** (say: pro-DOO-sur) is in charge of the budget, which is the money that goes into making the game. They also keep track of the schedule so the game is released on time.

A **video game tester** makes sure the game runs smoothly and does not have any issues before it's released. They play the game again and again . . . and again!

A **video game composer** (say: kum-PO-zur) creates music for the game. Music is important for setting the mood of a character or a level.

A **video game journalist** (say: JER-nuh-list) writes articles and reviews of video games. They usually work for magazines, newspapers, or websites.

A **video game translator** (say: TRANZ-lay-tur) changes the words in a game into another language. This way people all over the world can play the same games!